STORYTELLING FOR SMALL BUSINESS

CREATING AND GROWING AN AUTHENTIC BUSINESS THROUGH THE POWER OF STORY

Margaret Rode

STORYTELLING FOR SMALL BUSINESS
Creating and Growing an Authentic Business
Through the Power of Story

© 2018 by Margaret Rode and Websites for Good

Cover image copyright © Cargo / ImageZoo

CONTENTS

If you want to
change your life,
and if you want to
change the world,
you have to begin
with stories.

Gareth Higgins

INTRODUCTION

Mikaila Ulmer might have just decided to run a lemonade stand instead.

She could've sold her cool drinks simply by saying, "Try this. It's nice and cold and I think you'll like it. "Her neighbors in the hot Texas sun would've been refreshed. She'd have made a few bucks. And then she'd get back to the things eight-year-olds do.

But in that story, she wouldn't have ended up on TV, at the White House, or the teenaged CEO of a business whose products can be bought all over the country. Here's a better story, and it just happens to be true:

As a four-year-old, she'd been stung by a bee twice in the same week, and admits she hadn't handled it well. "After that I would freak out -- like overreact. My parents wanted me to learn more about bees so I would be less afraid. Doing that research I found out how incredibly important pollinators they were, and that they were dying." Her fears morphed into curiosity, then concern, and then helping bees became her mission.

Mikaila created a honey-sweetened lemonade using her great-grandmother's recipe, selling it at the Acton Children's Business Fair near Austin. She donated part of her profits to a charity that helps families in developing countries become beekeepers.

She told her story and shared her vision for helping bees with whoever would listen. It caught people's imagination. Slowly she grew a little business, brewing her lemonade for local events and local stores. By 2014, she had samples at Whole Foods Market. In 2015, then-10-year-old Mikaila appeared on the reality TV series Shark Tank. She convinced the tough judging panel to commit $60,000 toward building a business.

When she was invited to the White House in mid-2016, President Obama quipped, "I will be back on the job market in a few months, so I hope she is hiring." Mikaila's lemonade products are now sold in hundreds of stores across the United States under the brand *Me and the Bees*. She's still expanding, and still helping bees. (Listen to her inspiring tale at http://bit.ly/2n7USii.)

Mikaila had no MBA, no six-figure piggybank. She chose to leverage her passion, her vision, and the power of story to create something meaningful *and* profitable.

The best part? Everyone—*everyone*—reading this book has stories at least as compelling as Mikaila Ulmer's.

I hope this book will help you, my small business kindred, to gather them and share them. They'll help you create community, earn a good living, and grow the good work we're all trying to do.

2

HOW TO GET THE MOST OUT OF THIS BOOK

It's safe to say that anyone who'd buy a book with this title must have an interest in business storytelling. (Right?)

But I also recognize that not everyone is coming from the same starting point with it. Here are a few thoughts on how to get the most out of it, no matter where you're starting.

If you're new to the idea of storytelling in business:
You may just be intrigued by the concept of storytelling for your business and may be hoping for an overview and a little inspiration. If so, you might want to start with the brief introduction called **The story of story**. I'll walk with you through the basics of *why* you'd want to use story, then move into specific steps and examples.

If you're not yet sure how YOU would use it:
You may already know a bit about storytelling, but are stumped about how to do it for your business. Jump into **Isn't storytelling the same as marketing?** and/or **10 bedrock stories we can—and should—be telling** to learn more about that.

If you're already "there" and raring to go
And if you're looking for the nuts and bolts—specifics on diving right in and using story to connect with your people, start with **Setting the stage: Getting ready to tell your**

story. Then start scribbling in the Storytelling for Small Business Workbook (see below) and you'll start to see some amazing connecting stories unfold.

Don't forget to download the workbook

There is a free companion to this book, the **Storytelling for Small Business Workbook**, to help you capture your thoughts and story ideas as you read. It's a PDF file that can either be downloaded/printed and written into, OR saved to your computer to use as a fillable electronic document.

Download it here (PDF):
https://websitesforgood.com/workbook

3
THE STORY OF STORY

Story comes naturally to our species.

Human beings have been telling and gathering stories for tens of thousands of years. Storytelling comes as naturally to us as breathing.

We've always been story-creators and story-gatherers. Always. Imagine our ancestors sitting in a circle around a campfire. The clan doesn't have a written language to speak of, so all of life's critical lessons and choices come from the stories told in this circle: Which places to avoid walking alone. Where and how to catch your next meal without *becoming* a meal. Where to find those leaves that made the little girl-child's fever go away.

As you might imagine, the individuals who did the best job of telling and listening were the ones most likely to survive and thrive. (Which, coincidentally, is still true.)

Over the millennia, a lot has changed for us, but one thing hasn't: We're still a storytelling species. In fact, it's said that 70 percent of everything we learn in our lives is *still* learned through stories.

Story should come naturally to our businesses too.

My own work in online marketing puts me among purpose-driven people. I help them to gather and tell their stories so they can build a business that makes a difference.

But even if you don't consider yourself in that way, most of us want to have an authentic business with heart, integrity, and genuine compassion for the people we serve. We can't do that just by churning out one sales pitch after another; our stories are a much more fluid and natural way to get there than the latest marketing technique du jour.

But why did I write a whole book about this?

Because I'd like to invite us to once again step into the role of a storyteller, inviting people into our warm circle.

In the book I'll cover stories, ideas, and skills that have helped people shape their chosen work into both a force for good AND a livelihood.

Story isn't just another marketing tool. It's the most valuable traveling companion you can have in your business journey. Together we'll use it to connect, to earn and create trust, and to cultivate real relationships with the people you most want to reach.

Because the place where your story touches theirs is a place of pure magic and can change the world, a tiny spark at a time.

Sound good?

4
ISN'T STORYTELLING JUST MARKETING?

"We want people to connect with our people. We want folks to resonate with us and generally like us before they make the decision to work with us . . . we understand that hammering people with billboards and Facebook ads and marketing materials left and right won't lead to the clients we really want."

—Matt Cheuvront of Proof Marketing

What's the difference between storytelling and marketing?

To some, storytelling may be just another tool in the marketing toolkit, usually reserved for a quasi-moving origin story, a splashy client success story, or an impressive charitable campaign.

But I believe that, for a small business like ours, story goes far deeper than that. Done right and done honestly, storytelling is a way to create relationships with exactly the people you want to reach—the "clients you really want" as Matt Cheuvront says.

Metaphorically, it's a little bit like marketing's honest cousin. You know, the one that everybody likes. He's the one who pets every dog he passes on the street. The one who always remembers you can't eat shellfish. The one who asks, "Weren't you sick? Are you feeling better now?"

It's not trying to manipulate you and maneuver you into a sales box. It's putting yourself out there, letting everyone see your vocation, your values, and your wishes for the world. Believe it or not, that still matters nowadays.

What that *looks* like in the course of running a business or working for ourselves

I sometimes have to turn away folks who want to work with me. If I do, it's usually because our initial conversation has gone something like this:

"So," I ask. "What's your business? What do you do?"

They respond, "I've written this great guide called *You Can Get Rich in the Stock Market in Five Minutes a Day*. People are gonna love it. My son-in-law found you on Google. He says we should make a web page to sell the book, and then push out a bunch of ads, some pay-per-click, all that whatchamacallit sales funnel stuff that [*insert marketing thought leader-guru*] talks about."

[Margaret furrows her brow.] "Congratulations on your book. That's hard work. What's your goal? Why do you want to help the people who buy it?," I'll ask.

[Puzzled silence.] "Hey, look I don't know anything about this helping stuff. I just want to sell a shit-ton of books and retire. Is that a trick question?"

It's not a trick question. It's THE question.

First, let me make clear: In my book, there's <u>nothing</u> intrinsically wrong with wanting to make money. We're all businesspeople, after all. So it's not that.

It's just that I don't personally resonate with his story, which reads something like this: "Once there was a man who dreamed up a tactic he thought would help him to make as much money as possible from his audience, defined as anyone with a pulse and a PayPal account. The End." Combine it with some standard manipulative marketing tricks, and off he goes.

That's not really my thing. It may be yours, and if it works for you, that's A-OK. Mainstream online marketing tactics are all around us, and are used to great success in some cases. The gurus will tell you all about them. You just master the latest quasi-ethical "tripwire" system to get people to join a mailing list. You build a squeeze (sales) page with 27 vertical inches of sales pitch before you show the price. You craft a scarcity-based offering ("only 3 spaces left!") to goose people into making a snap judgment and buying quickly.

Lather, rinse, repeat.

I think of this way of doing business as "extractive." The marketer is focused on extracting maximum benefit from buyers by trading a service or product for the maximum price they can reasonably ask.

I, on the other hand, prefer to build a community full of good people based on mutual respect and support, with whom I'll have a lifelong—two-way—exchange of benefits.

Though it's all very common, there's one big problem with that plan: For most of the people reading this book, that's just really not who we are.

Here's who we are instead:

We have a skill, a gift, a product. We want it to find its way into the hands and minds of the people who need it most. We want <u>them</u> to get great benefit from it, and <u>we</u> also want to be able to earn a living by offering it.

We want this all to happen in a way that's decent, thoughtful, and human. We care too much about our people. We don't see our current and future customers as mere numbers on a spreadsheet.

So:

Marketing is using prescribed tactics to get as many appropriate people as possible to buy what you're offering.

Storytelling—telling yours, asking for others'—is a sustainable, honest way for small businesses to build a lasting community of resonant readers, buyers, clients, and fans.

It does that by being personal in a world that's becoming more impersonal by the hour. When you have the courage to tell your own story, it makes you real. It makes it clear that you're worth listening to. It shows you have a larger, longer-term vision that isn't all about "catching" them like fish in a net.

Inviting your people—clients and potential clients— to share their stories has the same impact. With that knowledge, you're able to create the most beneficial and helpful content, services, products, and systems for them. You can be there for them, in a world that rarely seems to take the time to care.

These folks are surprised and delighted to be treated like human beings. They go out and **tell your story to others in their social circles**. Those people become part of your community too. And so forth.

It's a natural process that *works*.

You can build a business that does well by doing good, surrounded and supported by people you care about ... AND you can earn a living doing it.

Imagine that.

It's a slower, more thoughtful form of "marketing," but you'll be building this house with bricks, not straw, and it'll be built to last.

5
STORY IS ALL AROUND US

We've watched for decades as big companies have spent billions on storytelling as a way to sell products. Think about Apple's "1984" commercial introducing the Macintosh. Chipotle's "Back to the Start" animated ad, illustrating their values around real food. Video stories of puppies and Clydesdales, which people share hundreds of millions of times. And virtually anything you see on TV during the Super Bowl.

These brands use stories to create an emotional attachment to their message. They know the old ways are changing. Traditional marketing, with its impersonal coercion, is losing its ability to move people. When it comes to getting people to sit still and pay attention, countless studies show that the tried-and-true tactics can't touch a well-crafted story.

So the big guys have been using the power of story for years. But sadly, our small businesses often overlook it entirely. Let's remedy that. Story can help us stand out in this weary, distracted, and suspicious world. Even more important, it can help attract the people we most want to talk to.

So, in a nutshell:

Storytelling connects. It's the way all people organize and find their place in the world.

It's how we understand our lives and work.
It's how we find common ground with other humans.

Let's talk about why this matters, and then ease our way into lighting up your own small business with story.

We'll start with the place where your story meets someone else's story, and something astonishing happens.

6
STORYTELLING AND THE CONNECTING POINT

Your stories matter.

If you run your own business, the willingness to share the stories behind your work can be incredibly powerful. In fact, in a crowded, noisy space like the online world, they're becoming the <u>only</u> things people pause long enough to listen to.

Your story: It doesn't matter if you're a coach, author, yoga teacher, hardware store owner, real estate agent, or artist: You have a story. It's what carried you from where you used to be to where you're standing right now.

Your audience member's story: The person to whom you want to offer your products, services, and wisdom—the one who's out there looking for you—also has stories that brought her here.

The connecting point, the spot where your storylines intersect, is a place of pure magic. When her story meets yours, a new one is created:

> **Theirs**: Once there was a woman (our Heroine) who dreamed of walking away from her wearying corporate life. She wanted to be a consultant for nonprofit organizations, but she feared she'd be worn down by

the demands of running her own business. She also felt paralyzed by all she didn't yet know. She couldn't move her feet forward.

Yours: *Once there was a life coach who'd once been petrified in the same way, and it really stunk. It stunk so badly, in fact, she chose to hang out a shingle and create some tools to help others vanquish those fears.*

The connecting point: *Our Heroine was finally able to find the courage to start her own business. Her nonprofit clients did amazing work that lifted up thousands of others. The Coach was able to continue helping more and more people, and build a joyful livelihood as well.*

And another:

Theirs: *Once there was a man (our Hero) who had always felt he had to hide the emotional pain of his lifelong depression. "Real men" didn't talk about such things. The weight of his hidden suffering cast a pall over his work, health, and relationships.*

Yours: *In the mythical land of Massachusetts, a wise writer had dug deep into his own experience with this kind of taboo pain. He'd been there. He found he had the gift of being able to articulate rock solid ways that men could use to begin defusing it for good. He wrote a book to share this with the world.*

The connecting point: The book's readers, including our Hero, were uplifted, and had a new lease on life. They responded with gratitude and positive reviews. They shared it with their friends. Both author and reader could move into their respective futures with more hope, peace and confidence.

What might you see as a possible Connecting Point Story for the work you do? Who's your hero(ine), and where might your stories touch one another's to create something bigger and better?

Story is a mighty tool to find your own connecting points, and create a new story with as many good people as possible.

7

WHY YOUR STORY MATTERS MORE THAN YOUR DATA

Most sales pitches lead with data.

Remember the gum that four out of five dentists used to recommend? Or the car model that's won annual awards from a famous auto magazine for five years running? Or which paper towel picks up a double-digit percentage more goo than the others? That's data, and it's long been an advertiser's go-to tactic.

But for people like us, in times like these, it turns out that stories carry more weight than facts and figures alone. They're more compelling than our science and our research and our string of credentials. Here are five reasons why:

1. Your story is far more interesting, and not only keeps people reading, but makes them feel good about it.

Ten years ago, they warned tech types like me that a website's home page needed to hook a reader within **10 seconds**. Miss that mark, and there was a very good chance readers would simply click away.

Nowadays we'd be downright gleeful if we had 10 seconds. Researchers at Missouri University of Science and Technology found that a visitor to your home page forms a first opinion of you **in less than two-tenths of a second**. It takes them just **another 2.6 seconds** to scan the page and either reinforce or contradict that first impression.

What does that mean for people like us, who use online spaces to get the word out about our work in the world? Your website or social media pages need to grab readers' attention quickly so that trigger-happy click finger will stand down.

That's good news for those of us who take story seriously. A ton of credible research over the past few years (funded by those big firms we've talked about—thanks guys!) has proven that our brains are far more engaged by storytelling than by facts alone. Start telling a story, and people are more likely to stick around to read it.

For example, if you're a consultant, your page *could* immediately pop up a graph showing the success trajectory of people who've worked with you. As a reader, I'd give it a glance and a respectful nod before I move on.

But if you lead with a snapshot—a story describing the before-and-after of someone you've helped go from troubled to tireless—I'll absolutely stay. On some level, I want to stick around and keep reading to see whether I find some tiny mirror-shard of my own situation in that story. And something crazy-great happens if I do:

That story will take up residence in a well-lit place in my mind.

It'll pop into my head while I'm waiting at the drive-up ATM, and my fingers will stop drumming the steering wheel.

It'll sneak its way into a conversation with a friend over lunch.

I'll get a flash of an image or a metaphor from the story while I'm waiting for the coffee to brew the next morning. I'll stare out the kitchen window and wonder how I'm going to get my *own* dream off the ground.

I'll come back to your website and see if there's a way I can learn more about what you do. (If you offer a free initial conversation, I'm the sort of person who'll be booking one.)

In addition to being "sticky" like that, story also quiets our distracted, hamster-wheel minds. It does that by inviting them to focus their full attention on absorbing the story and on making sense of it. As Jonathan Gottschall says in his book *The Storytelling Animal: How Stories Make Us Human*, "...In normal life, we spin about one hundred daydreams per waking hour. But when absorbed in a good story, we experience approximately zero daydreams per hour. Our hyper minds go still and they pay close attention."

So, to recap: Tell people a story and they'll listen. Show them you care about *their* story, so much so that you've created products & services just for them, and they'll naturally want to step closer and start a conversation with you.

It's our nature.

2. People *want* to be on your side, and want *you* to be on *theirs*. Story is what makes that happen.

We are wired for empathy. I think we've always known that, but modern research and behaviors are proving how true it is.

Picture every throat-closing, heroic tale ever shared on social media. The man who crawls out to rescue a dog from a freezing lake. The cop who adopts the child he saved from abuse. The philanthropist who uses her wealth to bring clean running water to a village for the first time.

Those stories are memorable, right? They hook into our brains and spread like viruses (hence the term "viral"). **We are hardwired for this**. We're wired to remember stories of people who've overcome, persevered, and shown courage for the right reasons. What they inject into us is this: *Life might be a mess sometimes, but hey, look! There's something good, something that matters. Being alive is still a good, good thing.*

That's why we shouldn't pigeonhole storytelling as just a persuasion or marketing tool. While it may indeed boost your bottom line, at the core of story lies the solid ground of genuine human connection. Because, as Seth Godin writes, "What we want in a low trust world is someone to trust." How we earn that trust as compassionate businesses is by cultivating integrity and by beaming this message out into the world:

You can trust me. Here's my story to show you why that's so. Because of my OWN experiences, I can truly, honestly see you. I understand what you've been through, and I can help you find what you've been looking for.

Show your audience an elaborate string of credentials or a seven-figure lifestyle, and it will impress certain people enough to follow you for a while.

But show your audience you understand them, and that you're a living, breathing human who has also overcome obstacles, and you'll build trust. That trust comes with the gift of a long-lasting relationship with those you most want to have in your life and work.

3. People want to interact with somebody who gives a damn about them.

I was sifting through my Facebook feed this morning when I saw this post from an online advertising firm:

> "...Customer engagement requires two components: behavioral analytics and engagement automation. We've combined them to introduce our new solution, Customer Engagement Automation."

Did you just get a little bit of linguistic vertigo? I know I did. You want to automate my *what*? Didn't I hear something like that in the Blade Runner remake?

Sorry. I don't mean to poke fun. (Yes I do.) There's so much wrong with this that I barely know where to start, and might not know when to shut up. But I'll try.

First, it's industry jargon common in the discipline known as Customer Relationship Management (CRM). It means, in a nutshell, "cool tools you can use to monitor and manipulate masses of people to buy your stuff without having to connect with them personally." If you're geeked out by this sort of jargon, I've just made your day. You're welcome.

But if you're not, let's talk.

This quote from the brilliant storyteller Annette Simmons has been scribbled across my office whiteboard for most of the year: "In our technological economy, human attention is the emerging scarce resource ... In today's world, almost anyone you want to influence is operating under a deficit of human attention."

In other words, we're already awash in "automation," unable to even consider keeping up with the information deluge. The one-two punches of overwhelm and depersonalization make good people feel lost and unimportant. We've <u>got</u> all the data we need. What we <u>don't</u> have is attention: Someone who cares enough to help us make sense of it all.

To begin creating more relationships, and be that one who helps the world make sense, I'd suggest a better recipe for attracting the perfect audience:

WHO: Decide exactly who you most want to help. (For an example of how I've done this, see my blog post <u>Who are you trying to help? Going beyond the ideal client exercise</u> to meet my client avatar, Jean)

WHAT: Create products, services, and resources that make the lives of these folks better.

WHERE: Promote yourself online because you genuinely care about their happiness and wellbeing, and want to help them as much as possible.

HOW: Build as many individual relationships as you can, so both you and "your people" see a spike in your respective happiness levels.

WHEN: Repeat. For the rest of your business's life.

Want to give this a try? Let's at least do the first element together—the **Who**.

Write down everything you think you know about the absolutely perfect client for you. These are the people who you could envision helping day after day, bringing good to their world, and never tiring of it. Describe them in detail, including their age, gender, vocation, and personality traits. (Make it up if you have to.) What things are most important to them? Where do they hang out? What do they watch/read? What single thing do they need most right now, in order to be happier?

Download the workbook. It makes this so much easier. Use the free companion to this book, the <u>Storytelling for Small Business Workbook</u>, to capture your thoughts as you read. Use the prompts in its *Your People* section to brainstorm. This one simple action—creating a client avatar or archetype—radically changed the trajectory of my business. I think it will do the same for yours.

Download a fillable workbook here (PDF): https://websitesforgood.com/workbook

4. The tide of resistance against traditional marketing tactics is rising, and frankly, most of them simply don't work anymore.

I still grumble about a TV ad I was unfortunate enough to see about seven years ago. (Just ask my husband.)

The CEO of a major consumer products company looked out from the screen and droned at me about their mission. It is, you'll be happy to hear, "to create products the consumer wants and needs."

Let's sidestep, for the moment, the issue of this being vague and meaningless. It would be like Nike stating their mission as, "To create things for people who like wearing shoes on their feet."

No, my core grumpitude came from the fact that he repeated the word "the consumer" at least four times. Around the fourth repetition I started to feel like an animated yellow mouth, mindlessly moving through the world chomping, popping pills, and devouring "products." It was like being in the same room with someone who's talking about you. *Dude, I'm right here.* I found it viscerally offensive: I am not just one-who-consumes. I'm a unique human being who matters.

Most folks who are online these days know what I'm talking about. We have a rapidly evolving sensitivity to BS, and resist being treated like a commodity or a walking wallet. We know the difference between someone who's being genuine and someone who sees us as a target for the latest "ethical bribe," "sales funnel," or "right hook."

We bristle when we see that the only part of our story that is of any interest to a marketer is the data he collects for his "customer relationship management" software.

What if people marketing a product or service started to treat us as though our individual stories mattered? What if, as journal facilitator and writer Barbara Stahura has provocatively stated, instead of simply having a story, we each ARE a living, breathing story? Clinical, dispassionate selling would become even more of a fading art form.

Here's a thought: **What if we just built as many mutually beneficial relationships with as many good people as possible, by learning and sharing one another's stories?**

5. Stories give you credibility, humanity, and approachability, breathing life into your facts.

Remember debate class in high school? Aristotle was either pleased or spinning in his grave at 5000 RPM as millions of teenagers squared up to a podium in scratchy dress clothes and framed their arguments with his principles. Remember what they were? **Ethos, Pathos, Logos**:

> **Ethos**, the ethical appeal, shows your credibility and character.
> **Pathos**, the emotional appeal, connects to your audience's emotions.
> **Logos**, the logical appeal, convinces your audience with facts and reason.

Story incorporates all three of these Aristotelian qualities into the recipe for making a connection with the people you most want to help.

An example of establishing this connection is through your website's About page, the best of which will utilize all three: **Ethos** is your credibility, which you show by way of your clarity and confidence in your area of expertise. **Pathos** is your 'how I got here' story—describing the road you walked to find your passion and calling. **Logos** is the nuts-and-bolts of your experience, maybe with a few judicious credentials.

(See the chapters **8 Easy Ways to Start Telling Your Stories Right Now** and **The One-Hour Story Jumpstart** to start creating a stronger bond between you and your audience quickly.)

By the way, none of this is to say you shouldn't bother to use facts and research. They play an important part too, of course.

But if you want people to stick around long enough to *read* them, breathe life into your facts with story. It will bring you to life in living color, and help you become someone they want as part of their lives.

Isn't that supposed to be at the core of every successful business?

8

START HERE: THE THREE ESSENTIAL QUESTIONS

What do you do?
Why do you do it?
And who do you help by doing it?

Anyone who's worked with my company, Websites for Good, will feel a twinge of recognition reading these questions. They're the ones I ask at the beginning of every new working relationship. In our wired world, they're fundamental.

Why? Well, imagine me as a potential customer/client you'd love to reach. I happen to need what you've got, and we're pretty much perfect for each other. In our magical world, Mr. Google can help me put my finger on any number of perfectly good products, services, or programs in a matter of seconds. Why should I stop searching, snap to attention, and choose yours?

It's because there's something in you that connects to something in me, so I feel like I've found exactly the right choice. There's an internal *click*. My eyes widen. I stop, sit back, and think, "Finally. Somebody who's nailed it, who GETS me and what I've been needing for so long."

You can't elicit that reaction with Gantt charts, popup windows, or the alphabet soup that may follow your name.

It comes from knowing the person you want to speak to, and knowing how you want to help them. *Before you ever open your mouth or type a word.*

So let's start again. I'm going to ask you to create three mini-stories:

Jot down the answers by hand or in the free, downloadable **Storytelling for Small Business Workbook**, available from the Resources section toward the back of this book, or from https://websitesforgood.com/workbook.

 NOTE: Don't be discouraged if these stories don't pour fully-formed out of your head like Athena right away. Once you get started, this stuff will come more and more easily, I promise.

What do you do? What—specifically—is your work in the world? How do you describe the unique set of services, products, education/wisdom, works of art, social change, etc. that form your work in the world? Tell us about that— the more detailed, the better.

Why do you do it? What's the story that brought you to this spot? What do you want to change for the better? What deeper "why" motivated you to brave the waters of self-employment or entrepreneurship? If this doesn't come easily, try starting a sentence this way: "I offer this because there's too much (or too little) X in the world." How would you complete the "X" ?

Who or what do you help transform by doing it? A certain slice of the human community needs what you're offering. You know who they are. Connecting with these specific people is the best possible outcome for you <u>and</u> for them. The alchemical reaction results in happier, healthier, smarter, or more empowered humans. So...who are they, and what's *their* story?

These are the three über-critical stories we all need to know inside and out if we expect our businesses to thrive. Write them. Know them. Be able to recite them in your sleep. Share them in as many ways as you can.

Together they form the rock-solid foundation of a long-term conversation with people whose values resonate with yours. The roots of your connected stories will sink far deeper than any modern marketing gadgetry ever could.

9

TEN BEDROCK STORIES WE CAN–AND SHOULD–BE TELLING

There are many possible stories you can be sharing to introduce people to your work and your business. I know it's not always easy to think in these terms, so with the examples that follow, I wanted to provide some inspiration to get you started.

Note that some of them are for big brands. That's okay. The very same kinds of stories are perfect for small businesses, private practices, self-employed folks, freelancers, and other modest-sized ventures.

In fact, stories from regular people like us may be even more compelling than those of our huge cousins. Stories about big-hearted corporations are nice enough. But many of us learn more and feel a stronger kinship with small, brave businesses that are still figuring it all out.

Let's start with the most common type of story you'll see online: The story of how you got started.

You Can Take "Your Turn" in the Storytelling for Small Business Workbook

You'll notice that all of these stories are followed by "Your Turn," prompts to help you use them yourself. The Storytelling for Small Business Workbook has pages in its 10 Bedrock Stories You Can Be Telling section to help you brainstorm the stories that bring heart, soul, and history to your work.

It's available from the Resources section toward the back of this book, or download a fillable PDF version from https://websitesforgood.com/workbook

YOUR ORIGIN STORY

What brought you here? Can you craft a concise story about the road that carried you to the work you do now? There are often fits and starts, clues and inklings, which may be old hat to you but which your readers will find very interesting. Here's one example I've long admired from a restaurant in my home state of Michigan:

Visit: http://mariecatribs.com/about/ to see more of this lovely story.

This is as far as one can get from the typical restaurant's dull "Here's our owner's impressive CV" page. A simple photoshow is made intriguing by a header that piques our interest: **"It's hard to imagine, but at one time Marie was banned from the family kitchen..."** A line like that draws us in, because we know this is not just another "I always wanted to make food" story. We're rooting for her as she tiptoes past her blind grandmother to make a mess in the kitchen.

Your Turn

Here are some questions you might consider in order to shape an origin story for your own work:

Was there some kind of clue when you were younger that this was something you wanted to do someday?

Why did you choose to do <u>this</u> work, rather than, say, becoming a taxidermist or a hula dancer or a Supreme Court justice? (with thanks for Martha Beck for that delightful imagery)

Was there an unlikely mentor somewhere along the way? An insightful (or terrible) teacher, neighbor, relative, friend, movie, song, historical figure, family pet?

Who tried to talk you out of it, and why? Why did you decide to do it anyway?
What hurdles, obstacles, or flaming hoops did you have to overcome along the way?

What specific series of events led to start doing the work you're doing now? How did your very first day of work in it feel?

WHY DO YOU GET UP AND DO THIS WORK EVERY DAY?

We live in a world of tremendous opportunity and seemingly endless freedom of choice about what we want to do with our lives. So why did you choose *this*? What problem are you solving by offering what you offer?

HISTORY

Warby Parker was founded with a rebellious spirit and a lofty objective: to offer designer eyewear at a revolutionary price, while leading the way for socially conscious businesses.

Every idea starts with a problem. Ours was simple: glasses are too expensive. We were students when one of us lost his glasses on a backpacking trip. The cost of replacing them was so high that he spent the first semester of grad school without them, squinting and complaining. (We don't recommend this.) The rest of us had similar experiences, and we were amazed at how hard it was to find a pair of great frames that didn't leave our wallets bare. Where were the options?

It turns out there was a simple explanation. The eyewear industry is dominated by a single company that has been able to keep prices artificially high while

---

Visit: https://www.warbyparker.com/history

The spark that created upstart eyewear marketer Warby Parker came when one of the founders lost his glasses on a backpacking trip. The cost to replace them was so high that he spent the first semester of grad school without them. Together they created an alternative to the big players that then dominated the eyeglass industry: "We believe that buying glasses should be easy and fun. It should leave you

happy and good-looking, with money in your pocket."
Perfect!

Your Turn

Here are some questions you might consider asking yourself to get into the spirit of the "why I do it" story:

Revisit your ideal reader/customer/client, and zoom in on the specific problem you're helping them to solve, whether it's "I can't afford healthy food" or "I don't know how to do my small business bookkeeping" or "I feel depressed all the time and don't know what might help."

How does the unique product or service you're offering enable something or someone to
...be more affordable
...be more attainable
...feel more beautiful
...feel happier or healthier
...suffer less pain/stress?

Using the term very loosely, what is your "competition" and how are you different?

WHAT'S YOUR BIGGER VISION?

Slightly different from the above, this is more focused on a story that leads to a larger positive change (for an individual, your community or the whole world). People want to know that you're not just taking their money and moving on to the next wallet. Paint them pictures of how you see the new, better story you're hoping for, for them or for everyone.

Spreading the Power of Optimism

LIFE IS NOT PERFECT. LIFE IS NOT EASY. LIFE IS GOOD.

We see it when we believe it. Each one of us has a choice: to focus our energy on obstacles or opportunities. To fixate on our problems, or focus on solutions. We can harp on what's wrong with the world (see most news media), or we can cultivate what's right with the world. What we focus on grows.

That's why the Life is Good community shares one simple, unifying mission: to spread the power of optimism.

Optimism is not irrational cheerfulness or "blind" positivity. It's a pragmatic strategy for approaching life.

Optimism empowers us to explore the world with open arms and an eye toward solutions, progress, and growth. It also makes life a hell of a lot more fun.

Optimism also enables us to access the ten most important tools we have for living a happy and fulfilling life. We call them the Life is Good Superpowers. But unlike X-ray vision, bullet speed, or Herculean strength, they are accessible to us all. The Life is Good Superpowers can help you overcome obstacles, drive forward with greater purpose, and enjoy the ride of life.

Visit: http://content.lifeisgood.com/purpose/

Clothing manufacturer Life is Good very clearly states that "...the Life is Good community shares one simple, unifying mission: to spread the power of optimism. Optimism is not irrational cheerfulness or "blind" positivity. It's a pragmatic strategy for approaching life."

Wow. I'm with them.

Your Turn

Here are some questions you might consider asking yourself:

What's askew in the world that your work or business or product helps straighten?

What's one aspect of it that you'd probably find a way to do anyway, even if you weren't earning income doing it?

What's one thing that changes for the better when someone works with you? Some sample answers for your clients, depending on your business, might include:

- Married couples re-learn to communicate without fear.
- Every home can feel more soulful or warm or safe.
- More people can work at home, saving fuel, travel time, and stress.
- Creative people can pursue their passions AND earn an income.
- Fewer people are burning out on the job.
- People are more optimistic about their retirement years.

...and so forth.

SHOW US WHAT YOU AND YOUR
NATURAL HABITAT LOOK LIKE

In our visual world, you're not "real" until people can see you. And haven't we all had enough buttoned-up annual report headshots to last us the rest of our lives? Tell the story of your humanity, your community, and your world. Show us your workspace (even if it's just a great coffee shop), your dog, your sense of humor, the place where you find your wildest inspiration. Show us You.

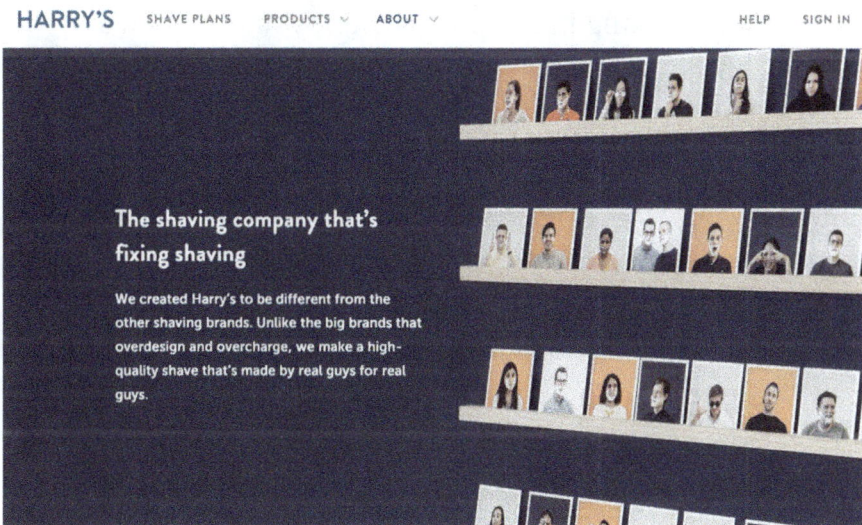

Visit: https://www.harrys.com/en/us/our-story

Shaving product maker Harry's website starts us out with a hilarious panel of each of its employees in full shaving lather (even the women). It goes on to show us the people who work in their German factory, closeups of the blades, even a 3D tour of the shavers. By the time you've traveled the site, you feel like you know these guys well, or at least wish you did. At that point, buying from them just feels right.

Your Turn

Below are just a few suggestions for things you might share to help bring people into your world. The social media site Instagram is worth a look if you have lots of visuals to share!

- Your storefront
- Your office, studio, workspace
- You, working in the place where you usually work
- The view from where you are at this very moment
- What you do to recharge your battery
- Your clients with you
- Where your products come from
- The faces of people who make them
- A video of your walk to work
- Your favorite work tools – even if it's just an awesome pen
- How you have fun
- Your dog, cat, hedgehog, or chameleon
- Different versions of you: Suit girl You, yoga pants You, mountaineer You
- Your family
- Your favorite object in your workspace

SHOW US YOUR AMAZING CLIENTS

Most stories revolve around a hero. In the stories you tell, more often than not, your hero should be your client. This isn't a brazen attempt to suck up to them (and shouldn't be). It's recognition that without them—without the story of what they want their lives to be like—you wouldn't exist. With their permission, tell the world how great they are, and feel the pride.

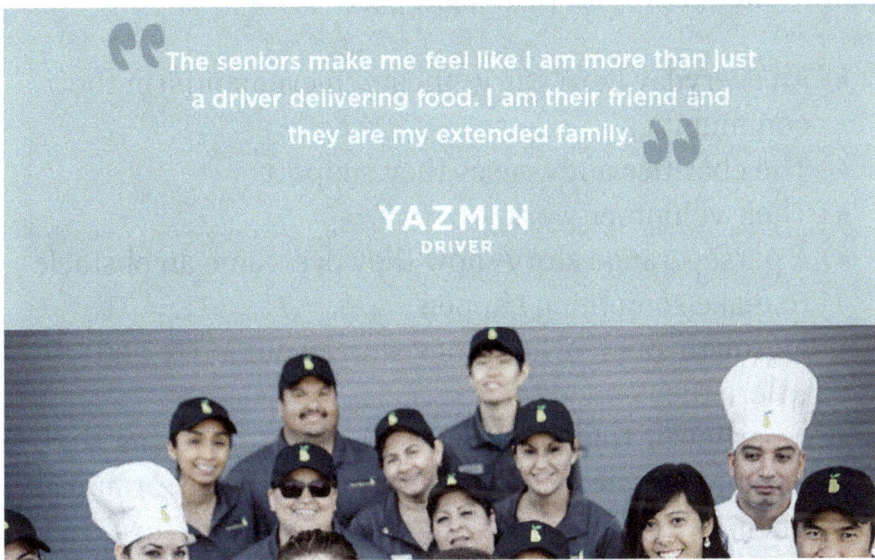

> The seniors make me feel like I am more than just a driver delivering food. I am their friend and they are my extended family.
>
> **YAZMIN**
> DRIVER

Visit:http://www.batemancommunityliving.com/meet-our-heroes

Bateman Community Living caters and delivers fresh, nutritious food to seniors. Their 'About' page sings the praises of both their dedicated staff AND the clients they serve. "At Bateman, we save lives every day. Many times it's the lives of our customers but truth be told, our clients also save us. They remind us of the importance of human connection and the positive impact we can create one meal at a time."

Your Turn

Many clients who have had a great experience working with you will allow you to tell their story. Make sure they know exactly how you're going to tell it, and if possible give them a chance to review what you'll say before it goes public.

Some "client hero" stories might be:

- An everyday hero story—their achievement(s) in their communities
- The charities and causes they support
- Their volunteer work
- A perseverance story—how they overcame an obstacle to make something happen
- A growth story—where they started out in life and where they ended up
- A particular trait that they demonstrate, such as optimism, generosity, creativity/innovation, or humor
- Their loves: Libraries, local art communities, fostering children, adopting shelter dogs, helping refugees

SHOW THE SOUL AND HISTORY BEHIND YOUR PRODUCT, CRAFT, OR SERVICE

People love to know that the thing they're holding in their hand, or the service they're about to pay money for, has a life story of its own. If you're an artist, show where your piece is made, and how. If you make natural skin products, show where the ingredients come from. If you're an author or a coach, show us the history or place(s) that inspired you. No limits!

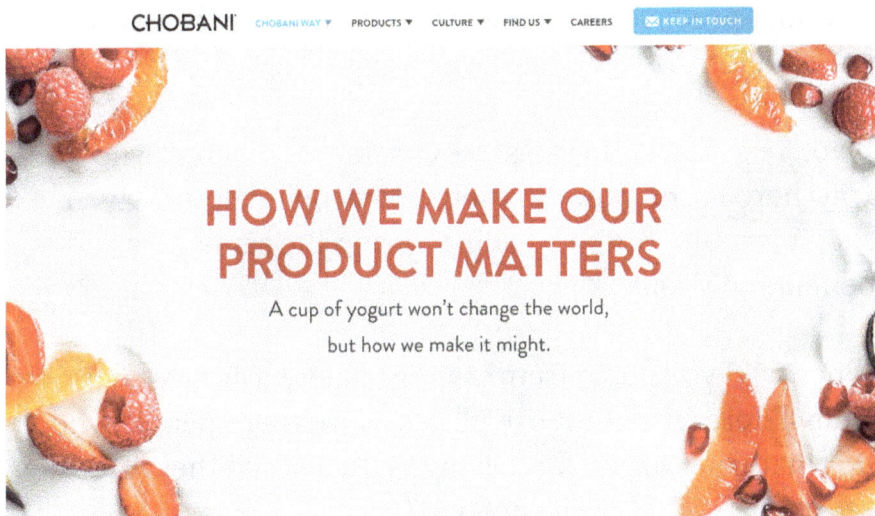

Visit: http://www.chobani.com/story

Yogurt manufacturer Chobani's "Our Craft" page is a glorious, colorful storybook celebrating the ideals behind their product, the admirable sourcing of their ingredients, and their sustainable manufacturing practices. Their "Story" page tells the story of the company's Turkish founder Hamdi Ulukaya, and how he went from a child of seminomadic dairy farmers, to (clueless) businessman, to entrepreneur & philanthropist. (And by the way, did you know that "Chobani" is a variant on the Turkish word for "shepherd"? I didn't.)

The Chobani website is a treat for story-lovers.

Your Turn

Some things you might consider sharing with your audience:

If you sell a product, what is its history? What were its "product predecessors" – what did people use before, to perform for the same task?

If you're a coach, therapist, counselor, or mentor, who are <u>your</u> heroes and how did they help people? How are you shaping your work to be able to bring the same gifts and benefits to peoples' lives?

Where did you come from? Where did your family come from before that? In those places, were there people who do what you now do for a living? What would they/DO they say about your chosen vocation?

If you could have an imaginary conversation with your great-great-grandmother and explain your work/business to her, how would you explain it? What would you compare it to, in her world?

TELL US A STORY ABOUT THAT TIME YOU REALLY MUCKED THINGS UP

Yep. It's strange and counterintuitive, but we trust people more when they show us they're not infallible. If someone is perfect and has never taken a misstep in her life, how can she possibly understand us? I'm a big fan of people who admit they've stumbled, but then learned a valuable lesson, brushed themselves off and kept going.

the innocent timeline

This is where the story is told and old fashion mistakes are exposed. Click and drag your way along, or just use the nice arrows. To read a particular story, click on any of the pictures.

| :hing for the :all room | how to go bankrupt, quickly | bigger, faster, waterier | a proper knee: in the park |

Visit: http://www.innocentdrinks.co.uk/us/our-story

Innocent Drinks, for example, published a timeline of its steps and missteps from its inception to now, including the data point "how to go bankrupt, quickly" ("...We give 46% of all profits to charity and nearly bankrupt the business...") Fun, real, and informative.

Your Turn

Here are some thought-starters for capturing your most hair-raising mistakes . . . and how you bounced back:

- Your first "office." Mine was a recycled schoolteacher's desk in a spare bedroom that was so cold in the winter I worked wearing a parka and fingerless wool gloves.

- One thing you wished you'd known when you started

- An example of hiring exactly the wrong person (oh so very, very wrong) and how you learned from that

- The well-intentioned advice others have given you that you either accepted (and possibly regretted) or ignored (ditto)

- A before-and-after description of your product/ service THEN, and your product/service NOW

IF YOU HAVE A "PARTNER STORY," LET'S HEAR IT

Do you work with other smart, compassionate businesspeople for greater impact? You can tell a story about something you learned from another marketer, and how it ended up benefiting you both. Or how about one in which you cooperated or collaborated to help solve a sticky problem, and gave one another credit? Craft beer fans may remember this one:

Visit:https://averybrewing.com/beers/collaboration-not-litigation-ale

Ten years ago, Avery Brewing (Boulder, CO) and Russian River Brewing (Santa Rosa, CA) discovered that they were each making a beer called Salvation. The founders decided that, rather than go through litigation, they'd brew a collaboration beer. The result was a popular beer they called Collaboration Not Litigation -- a blend of both beers that was first brewed in 2006 and has been made almost every year since.

Your Turn

Not everyone has a collaboration/partnership story, but it's worth exploring.

Think about other businesses/individuals you've hired, or that you've been hired by. Was there a mutual benefit or sweetly unexpected outcome you realized by working together?

Did you start your business with an overdeveloped sense of competition, hoping to "one up" people who do or sell the same thing(s) you do? Have you ever had an epiphany that led to cooperating with the very same person you used to resent?

Have you ever recommended another business you trust, or been recommended? How'd that go? What were the unexpected outcomes?

Have you been part of a mastermind group, co-working space, or networking organization that's led to a surprising connection?

TELL US ABOUT THE 'HELPERS' YOU SUPPORT

"When I was a boy and I would see scary things in the news, my mother would say to me, 'Look for the helpers. You will always find people who are helping.' "

—Fred Rogers, Mister Rogers' Neighborhood

The media is full of stories of conflict and fear. People are anxious to hear good stories. Show us how you help the helpers. Tell us about your pro bono work, volunteerism, charitable giving. Show us another dimension of your character and values. Good people like to support, buy from, and do business with other good people.

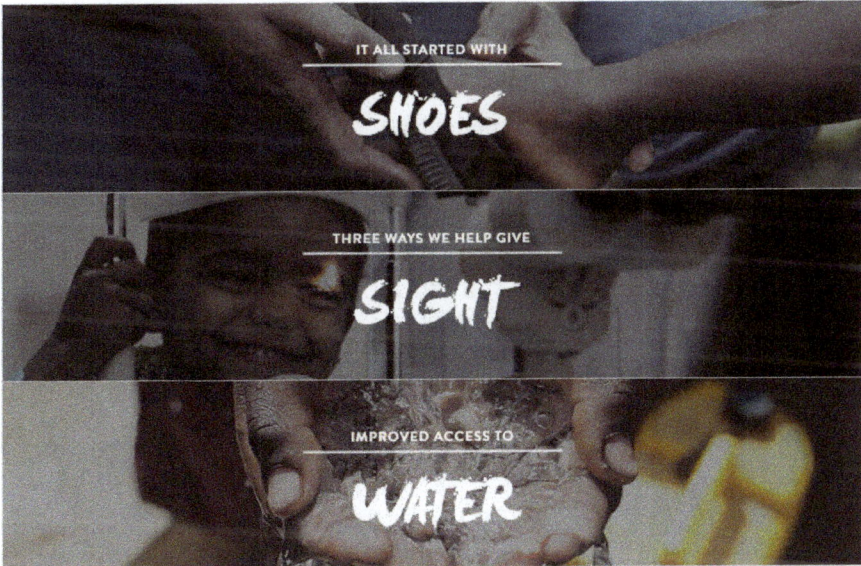

Visit: http://www.toms.com/improving-lives

With every product purchased, shoe manufacturer TOMS pledges to help a person in need via their One for One® program. Consumer purchases fund charitable giving in 70+ countries around the world by giving shoes, restoring sight with vision surgeries, providing safe water, and more. TOMS keeps evolving, monitoring their programs to continue to ensure their charity work effective, innovative, and locally-based.

Your Turn

In working with compassionate businesses, I've never yet met a person who didn't have a charity, cause, or local effort they supported, either personally or professionally. What's yours? Help people to know that you're part of something bigger. Here is a thought-starter list:

- Donating a portion of profits to a specific charity
- Bringing your skills, labor, or knowledge to local social programs
- Supporting efforts to squash something patently evil, such as child trafficking
- Teaching free workshops/classes in your community to help people learn a valuable skill or perspective
- Setting up internships for new college graduates, or hiring locally even when outsourcing to offshore freelancers might be cheaper
- Offering your product or service as a 'reward' for those who are giving of themselves in some way in the community

SHARE WHAT YOU DO, AND WHAT YOU DON'T...AND WHY

More than anything, this kind of story can give your small business a personality. It can show your commitment to your core offerings and core values, and demonstrate that you're serious about your chosen work. Or, it could just present you as smart or funny or approachable, as with Humaan.com's example:

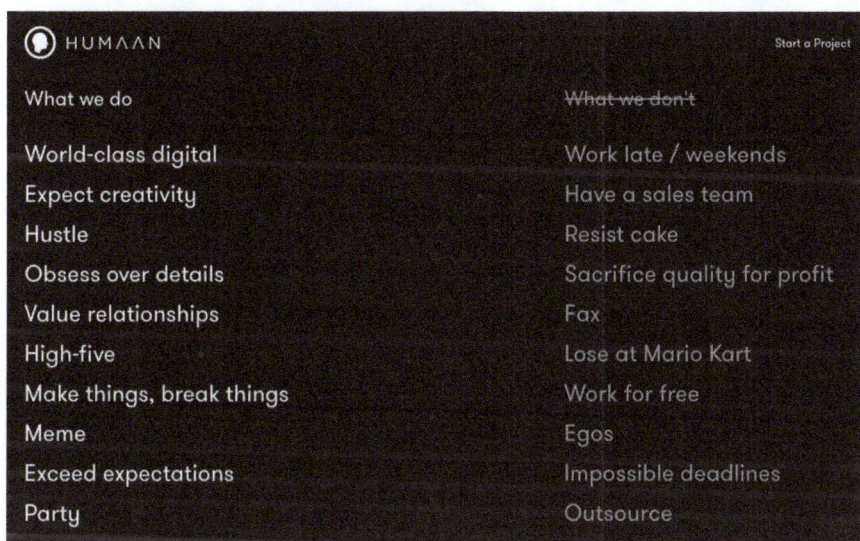

What we do	What we don't
World-class digital	Work late / weekends
Expect creativity	Have a sales team
Hustle	Resist cake
Obsess over details	Sacrifice quality for profit
Value relationships	Fax
High-five	Lose at Mario Kart
Make things, break things	Work for free
Meme	Egos
Exceed expectations	Impossible deadlines
Party	Outsource

Although we all try so hard to achieve some kind of perfection and infallibility in the public's eye, most people actually feel more comfortable with people who have a few quirks, and who have a sense of humor about them. Don't be afraid to have a personality, to show what you are and what you aren't. Your true people will gravitate to you.

Your Turn

Share a bit of yourself that will help "your people" feel like they know you better. Here are some questions you might consider asking yourself:

What do you do well? What would earn you a medal in an afterlife?

What do you completely and utterly stink at doing?

What's your Myers-Briggs type (MBTI) or another personality type, and what does it allege you're like...versus what you're *really* like? Show us the pigeonhole you've flown from. The Myers-Briggs prayers always make me laugh. The one for my type, INFJ, is "...*please help me not be a perfectionist (wait...did I spell that right?)*"

Are you an introvert whose idea of a perfect day is good coffee, cashmere socks, and a doorbell that doesn't ring? Or a flaming extrovert who strikes up a conversation with every UPS delivery person, barista, or potted plant?

Have fun with this. Celebrate yourself, and the fantastic diversity of our world.

10

INVITE AND CELEBRATE THE STORIES OF YOUR AUDIENCE

Wherever possible, **your client, customer or community member should be the hero of the stories you tell.** That generally requires you to know a bit about what they're up to. How well do you know the members of your 'tribe?' Do you know their stories?

In my experience, most people with small businesses have trouble describing the people they hope to reach and engage with. When I ask them "Who's the person who most needs what you're offering?" and "What is their story?" I often learn that they have only the roughest of ideas.

Oh, they know their *own* end of things. They know they have a good product or a valuable offering that will help certain people in a tangible way. But they often can't clearly *see* those people, or what's important to them.

Here's an example: Say you're a coach or therapist who specializes in working with a specific population (e.g. people in transition, suffering from eating disorders, having trouble with relationships, or burning out from their job). You may envision having a chat with them, asking "How can I help?" You might think they'll answer:

"I'm in transition. Can you help make it easier?"

A fair guess. But in reality, their story might sound a lot more like this:

> "I've always been able to figure things out. I grew up in a family of self-sufficient people, and I knew how to take care of myself AND my siblings. But since my own youngest child went off to college, I'm off the rails. I can't sleep more than a few hours at night, I feel angry all the time, and my husband and I barely speak to each other. I don't know what to do to get back to the happy person I used to be."

Most people <u>want</u> to be the hero of their own story. They may recognize that something's changed, and that something's going on that isn't okay with them. They want to return to the calm, self-aware problem-solver they took pride in being before, and want to move through life's ups and downs with grace. *They may not know what to call it, but they know what they need.*

Here's another example, if you're in a business like hospitality (restaurants, hotels, travel):

It might just be,

> "I'm looking for a boutique hotel in San Diego."

But it might be instead,

> "I've just worked 50 consecutive 60-hour weeks and I'm so exhausted I can't even spell it. I have

nightmares about teetering towers of files all around me. I want to spend a few days in a place where someone's caring for me as well as I usually take care of everybody else in my life. I want to walk to a nice Italian restaurant, and spend time where I can hear the ocean. I want people to be nice to me, like they're actually glad to see me. I'm hoping I can recharge and go back to my work with the passion and energy I had a year ago."

And yet another, if you're an artist or craftsperson:

It's not just,

"I want a pretty table for my apartment."

It's probably also,

"I'm tired of mass-produced junk. I want to look at the things in my house and know that a real-live human made them. I want to feel like I'm supporting my community, supporting a small business, and supporting someone's passion. The world feels so impersonal now, like we just don't care about each other anymore. I want to get off that train."

Your readers, clients, buyers, and donors are rich characters, heroes-in-the-making of their own lives.

Spend some time with the questions below, or see if you can come up with your own that truly bring "your people" to life for you.

Who—specifically—are the people that you are trying to reach?
Go beyond a two-word phrase or bullet-point list of traits. Build us a character. Not "single moms," but "single moms who are money-stressed and time-stressed but who know they want to create a specific life experience for their child." Not "healthcare professionals," but "healthcare professionals who are burned out, out of balance, and badly in need of a plan to get back their clarity and return to the job they love."

What are specific challenges they've faced in the past few days or weeks? (as it pertains to the issue you're here to help them with)
What are their hurdles?

What could their future look like if you could help get those hurdles out of their way?
What—again, specifically—are you offering them that will give them more delight, more confidence, more inspiration or more hope for their future?

What's the story you want to help them create?
How does their personal/professional life change, and what's the specific "moment of deliverance" that shows the change? *How can you help them be the hero of their own life, or company, or family?*

An Example Story: Meet Jean

Here is an example of a typical composite story I created out of the countless audience stories I've gathered over the years. I revisit it again and again as I try to use my own small business to help as many people as possible:

She's a restless corporate executive who tried hard to fit in, but found herself staring into her coffee cup most mornings, thinking there must be something more meaningful than taking home a paycheck and adding to an employer's bottom line. Finally, with a little money she's been squirreling away, she turns her back on the 9-to-5 life and heads down the path to self-employment, where she starts a coaching business (or yoga studio or pet sitting service or graphic design firm or...) She gets some help from a coach to create some service offerings. She goes out to VistaPrint or Moo and has some simple business cards made up. She joins the local chamber of commerce. And then...cue the sound of crickets.

Other businesspeople tell her she needs a good website, social media, all of that. She doesn't really know where to start, or how to even begin wading through all the options, choices, and conflicting information, so she freezes up and procrastinates. She tries a few things to get customers directly. She networks. She teaches a workshop at the local rec center and two people show up. She spends a lot of time with her face in her hands at night.

I work with different versions of this person every day. I devote my life's minutes to helping them get the word out about their work, because I believe heart-based, authentic businesses are the hope for our questionable human future.

But I can only help them because I carry them in my mind's eye all day.

If you have direct contact with current or future clients, you might be able to gather stories just by asking questions. They may take the form of:

Testimonials and tales of change
If your work or product has changed someone's life for the better, ask for that story and share it. The more heartfelt, authentic, and <u>specific</u> these are, the more power they carry.

Customer service stories...and more
I learned about the fantastic visual storyteller Branden Harvey through a feature in the Southwest Airlines in-flight magazine. He told the story of how Southwest helped him connect and fall in love with his now-wife Sammi, who lived halfway across the country. The airline's video storytelling culture is a virtual guidebook to telling this kind of story: https://www.youtube.com/user/NutsAboutSouthwest

Photos that are worth a thousand words: Your website and social media channels (especially Instagram) are terrific places to share photos of your customers enjoying your product, wearing your art, in conversation with you, doing something they couldn't do before your stories intersected, and generally having a more wonderful life. Check out little Letterfolk.com and their great way of sharing how their product is used.

Celebrating your customers' successes: If your clients, customers, readers or fans have something to celebrate—

especially something your work together might have had a hand in—crow about it. Show how proud you are of their award, published book, website, job promotion, health milestones, whatever makes you smile.

Learning and sharing the beautiful true stories of the people you're trying to reach can be hugely, tremendously rewarding, and will transform your communications like nothing else can.

11

SETTING THE STAGE: GETTING READY TO TELL YOUR STORY

When you're getting ready to tell a story, you want to be sure that people are listening. That means setting the right tone and creating the right atmosphere. After all, who tells a spooky Halloween ghost story amid bright fluorescents and with "Don't Worry Be Happy" blaring?

Let's set the stage for story by adjusting some simple aspects of your website and social media to be more welcoming to your ideal audience member.

Check your colors

Choose colors that create the right feel and the right emotional connection with your unique reader.

Color can create mood. For example, if you're trying to tell a story that calms and quiets the stressed people who come to you for help with anxiety, loud reds and oranges probably aren't the right choice (unless perhaps it's a photo of a walk through an autumn forest). Heavy use of blue and gray tones can give a strictly-business impression. Earth tones can be soothing and quiet. Yellows can lend an uplifting feeling. And so forth. Google "Adobe color wheel" to see examples of different color palettes and the impression they might give (great for visual types like me).

On a website, this can be controlled by adjusting things like the color of the text headings, lines, bullets, backgrounds, and the predominant colors taken from the images you use.

On social media, though you do have some control over the basic framework's colors (for example, by changing Facebook's cover photo/banner at the top) you can best control the dominant colors the viewer sees by photo choices.

Check for highly readable and appropriate typography

Larger, clearer text and uncomplicated fonts (typefaces) will help people quickly and easily read & understand where you're going and what you're offering. Don't make them squint or struggle with tiny, gray-on-white type, or assault them with frilly, overly complicated curly fonts. I like this interactive page of Google font pairings so I can see how the most readily available fonts look together: http://fontpair.co.

In terms of font sizes, peoples' preferences are changing, and more of them prefer larger sizes than a few years ago. If setting your type in pixels, try to keep your font size above 14px or 16px, with 150% line spacing.

Make liberal use of photos, video or other engaging imagery

Our minds process visuals many times faster than they do text. If your website or social media is mainly vast stretches of plain text, no matter how compelling it is, I'd ask you to reconsider. It's much better to visually break up a page by including photos, pull quotes, illustrations, or other visuals that support your content.

Read on to **8 Easy Ways to Start Telling Your Stories Right Now** for a more detailed description of why and how visuals can make your online presence more effective, as well as free sources and strategies for finding the right photos.

Use negative space to focus the reader's attention properly

We've all seen websites with every square millimeter of screen real estate crammed with content. Gargantuan blocks of text, charts, buttons, ads, and dozens of graphics compete for attention. Sites like this are claustrophobic and visually stressful to navigate. (Imagine a home jammed tight with furniture pieces, artworks, area rugs, and other decorative detritus covering everything, with only the narrowest spaces left to squeeze through. Does that sound like a relaxing place to make an important decision?)

Building in negative space—also called whitespace—creates areas where readers can easily see where one thought ends and the next one begins.

Having more visual breathing room tends to better focus readers' eyeballs on what IS there, allowing them to travel calmly and naturally from one part of your message to another.

Be clear about what people can do to keep reading

Remember that you're telling a story with everything seen on the page, not just the words. You need to make sure people know how to go to the next "chapter." Use clear buttons, arrows, icons, color changes, and transitions to make it 100% clear to readers what to do next at any given place.

Even the smallest amount of frustration about what to do or where to go can try their patience—and they may shrug and leave your website.

Double-check your copywriting and tone to be sure they convey <u>your</u> voice and personality

Here's an exercise I like to do: Sit down with a friend, family member, client, colleague, or even your cat. Pour a cup of coffee and then read your website's home page or your social media material out loud to them, as though it's part of a conversation. (Bonus points for recording yourself with your phone, and then playing it back.)

How do the words sound coming out of your mouth? How do your headlines sound? Natural? Comfortable, with the right degree of formality (or none at all?) Or does it sound stuffy, stilted, overly formal, impersonal, or like someone else's voice? Don't try to emulate or imitate.

The best stories are told in YOUR voice—the voice you'd use to talk with a real live human being.

12

EIGHT EASY WAYS TO START TELLING YOUR STORY RIGHT NOW

1. Give your About section or page a rethink.

One of the easiest starting points for building story into your online presence is the "About" text on your website or your social media profiles.

More than just a place to sway people with your credentials and your awards, this is also a space to show parts of you that allow readers to understand, trust, and root for you. This space has endless possibility, but might include:

- How did you get here? Give a super-brief but descriptive timeline of how you came to be doing what you're doing.
- Why do you do this? Tell a story about an event or epiphany that made you choose this path.
- Give an example of who you help, and HOW you help, and why.
- Describe a short snapshot of your life – a bit about your current life that someone in your audience might resonate with. This can be warm, or brave, or simply funny, though I <u>wouldn't</u> suggest going as far as novelist Robert Rankin: "*A retired Tupperware salesman, he divides his time between wearing old straw hats, collecting whales and commuting between the planets. His wife is tall. Very tall.*"

- Bonus points: Visualize someone in your ideal audience chatting with a friend over coffee. S/he's telling the friend about you. You can hear your reader telling a story that illustrates why they feel good about working with you or buying from you. The friend arches her eyebrows and says, "Wow. That's freaking amazing." What is the story she's just told? What makes you different, better, for the people you want to reach?

2. Start writing a blog.

Yes, even if it's something you've avoided so far. (And if it is, see the websitesforgood.com blog post **10 reasons to consider writing a blog, even if the thought of it makes you cringe**)

A blog is a place where you can literally tell stories until the cows come home—in fact, the more interesting, the better. Long ones, short ones, photographic ones, video posts, testimonials, results, a few juicy confessions, workshops you presented or attended, lessons learned, valuable tools you discover, people delightedly making use of your product/service/knowledge, bits of poetry or wisdom... it all combines to create a fantastic space where people can learn ABOUT you and FROM you.

A blog is also uniquely suitable as an automatic archivist of the growth of your work, not to mention that it's the perfect vessel for easily sharing your voice with any social media outlet with just a click or two.

3. Add more of the right photos or videos.

A single photo can tell a story without any words at all, or with very few. Have a look at this one:

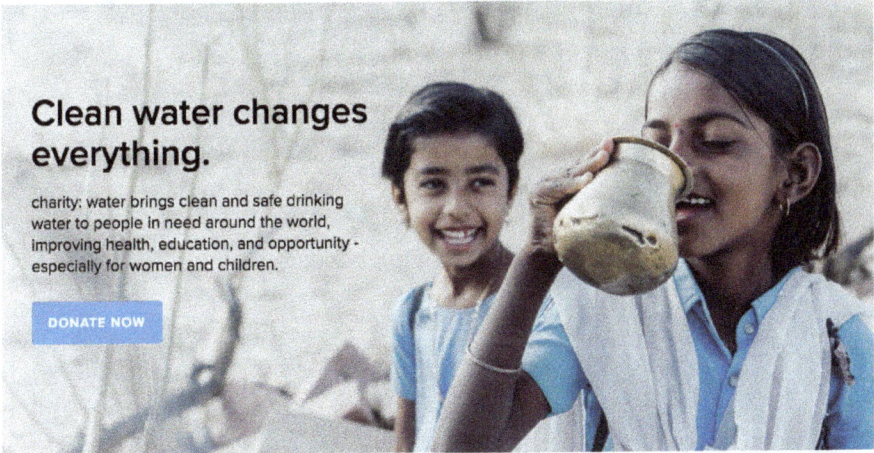

Clean water changes everything.

charity: water brings clean and safe drinking water to people in need around the world, improving health, education, and opportunity - especially for women and children.

DONATE NOW

Source: https://www.charitywater.org/

This site, charity: water, is one of the best examples of storytelling that you can find on the web. Rather than a pageful of statistics on what percentage of kids miss school or go thirsty, they use a simple image of girls in school clothes, in front of a backdrop of mayhem, able to at least hang out together and have a drink of water.

The headline and text explain the campaign, and a "Learn More" button below takes the reader to the guts of the issue. But it's the image that does all the heavy lifting: It drops you right into the action and makes your brain want to click that button to read the whole story.

(Trigger alert: If you're reading this and you're hungry, skip over this next example so you won't be tempted.)

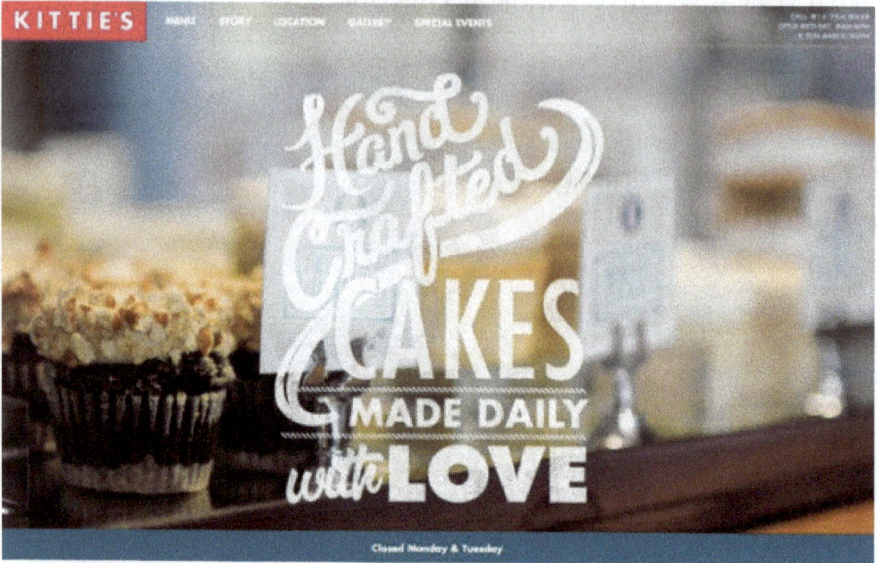

Source: https://kittiescakes.com/home

This image needs absolutely nothing else to get the story across for this small bakery in Columbus, Ohio. I can see the beauty of the cakes and cupcakes. I know the heart of their story from the just even-word explanation: All is made by hand and fresh ("made daily"), by someone who dares use the "L" word ("with Love") out loud to refer to their products.

For images that move you and will move your audience, getting to know a local photographer who can shoot exactly what you need can be a brilliant investment. Barring that, get acquainted with good-quality stock photo houses like pixabay.com, unsplash.com, and pexels.com. Learn to search for images you are permitted to reuse at places like Flickr.com, Wikipedia, Creative Commons, or Google. For many tips and sources, see our blog post Finding the Right Images Without Brain Damage.

4. Consider using illustrations.

Illustrations have all the visual advantages as photos, but with even more range and flexibility. Illustrations can make hard-to-explain concepts easier to digest, and can combine different elements of your story with things like step-by-step instructions, diagrams, maps, or directions. Check out Evernote's use of illustrations to explain how their product works for you. Product shots are combined with clear, 2- to 3-word headings that each support the main story: "With this product, you can capture and be able to remember the most important stuff in your life."

Source: https://evernote.com (archival)

You can have illustrations created by a graphic designer, try your hand at DIY-ing it with http://canva.com, or peruse http://fiverr.com for help with simple graphic tasks.

5. Think about background images behind your text.

I love background colors and images for setting a scene. If you're telling a story, large "hero" photos and background images can bring your viewer right into the heart of your world.

Notice how Ruffwear (adventure gear for dogs) connects its website sections with the "idea" of a journey, with a moving dotted line telling the story of finding an adventure with your furry pal. Even the email sign up box is not just a solid color with some writing superimposed, but a large smile-provoking image and a background pattern that is actually a faded topographical map. The heart of adventure!

IMAGINE BEING A DOG.

Not just any dog, mind.

A dog with boundless energy and so much drive, you struggle to fit into normal family life. You can't help it. You mean well. You're just a little crazy (in a good way!). Unfortunately, this makes you "difficult to home" and means you might spend your whole life in a shelter.

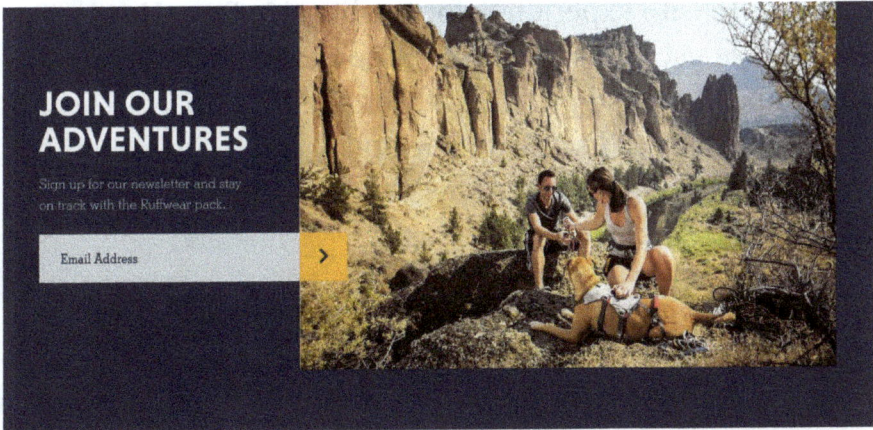

Source: https://ruffwear.com

Graphic design elements like these can help tell your story and bring your audience right into it...without you having to say a word.

6. Embed a video.

Adding video, either as a background effect or as an engaging, watchable piece of your story, can bring your website or social media to life.

To use one of our own examples, we wanted to create a tranquil website experience for the hospice Enso House. To do that, we used a background video of their beautifully contemplative pond prominently on the home page. The gently moving leaves and quiet ripples on the surface of the water truly tell the story of this peaceful, unique place—in a way mere words could not:

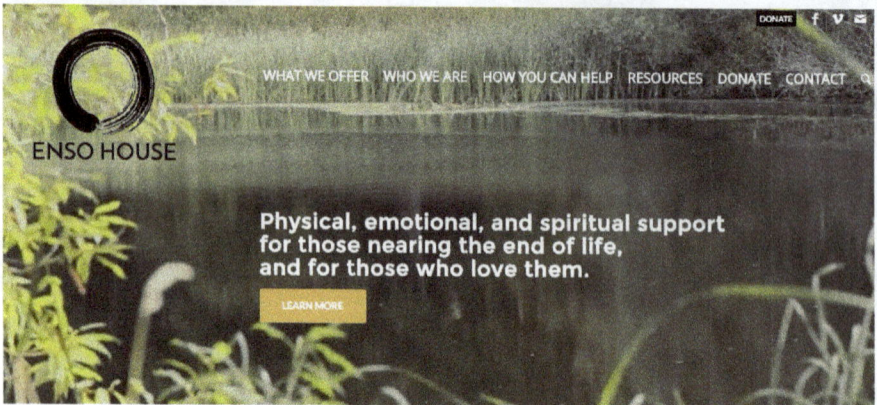

View video at: http://ensohouse.org

7. Explore the social media channels that tell your story the best...and that your ideal audience members frequent too.

I know a local corporate-type-turned-artisan who makes wonderful soaps, scrubs, oils, and even teas. Her creations are terrifically photogenic, and I've encouraged her to explore Instagram and Pinterest. Photos of her beautiful bath crystals and rosemary- and flower-studded soap bars are irresistible, and she can easily shoot and post them herself. This adds another place where people can find and fall in love with her products.

Social media giant Facebook has been giving preferential treatment to posts that include video, which has been a boon for people who like to learn that way. In fact, when asked where Facebook would be in five years in terms of mobile and video, Facebook VP Nicola Mendelsohn said the social network would "probably" be "all video."

Do you have an "explainer" video where you tell the story of your service or product or philosophy? A video of your shop or restaurant or art studio? A how-to video with step-by-step instructions on doing something your audience finds useful? If you haven't done it already, think about dipping your toe in those waters. You don't need an expensive camera or a cinematographer to give it a try and see how it feels and how it's received by your audience.

In fact, if the nature of your business lends itself to telling stories with video, consider setting up a YouTube channel to corral them all in one place (from which they can also be easily beamed right into your website pages and other social media if you so choose).

8. Add testimonials (stories) from those who love you.

How is a testimonial a story? A statement from someone who's had a positive experience with you is a heroic partner story in a pint-sized package.

Testimonial stories often share a similar plot line: "I was here at point A, and wanted a change. I found (you!) and some real magic happened. Things are so much better here at point B."

Although we've all seen examples of testimonials that sound hollow, a genuine, heartfelt, complimentary testimonial from a real human being (even with a tiny photo) can add a powerfully personal element to your website or social media.

See more about that in the next section, The One-Hour Story Jumpstart.

13
THE ONE-HOUR STORY JUMPSTART

There are tons of ways to get started using story to improve your online communication and your client connections. You've just seen a sampling of them in **8 Easy Ways to Start Telling Your Stories Right Now**.

But I know I'm not alone in wanting to try out something bite-sized to see whether it excites me or not.

So grab a pen and some paper (or open a new, uncluttered document on your device) and let's take a bite together.

STEP 1: Identify who's listening to you (5 minutes)

Turn off all your devices and distractions and sit quietly, preferably a place where you won't be disturbed.

Close your eyes and take three very deep, relaxing breaths. Exhale as fully as you can, bringing more fresh oxygen into your body on the next inhale.

Now, in your mind's eye, sit your ideal audience member/client/customer down in front of you. We'll call them your Listener. Imagine you two are sitting somewhere that's comfortable and natural for both of you: Your comfy office or studio, a coffee shop, on a park bench, on a boardwalk near the sea, on a sunny window seat somewhere ... wherever feels right.

Who is that person? And if you asked them, how would they explain why they've come to talk with you? Let them tell their story. To capture this for your own frame of reference, jot it down in a few words. Examples:

A person trying to cope with chronic pain
A life coach just starting out and feeling frustrated
A healthcare professional burned out on the career she loves
An artist or author or maker who hates the business side of business
A mother of a differently-abled child who's stressed
A new homeowner trying to make their home greener
A nonprofit leader needing to boost visibility and/or donations
A person just diagnosed with cancer and feeling shell-shocked
A small businessperson who doesn't want to do shifty marketing
A person with debilitating anxiety who's tried everything
A couple who can't seem to stop arguing
A stay-at-home dad seeking connection and community

Smile at your Listener. Keep them in your mind's eye as you move to the next step.

STEP 2: Give their need a noun (5 minutes)

If you could gift your Listener with anything through your work, what would it be? Think of a noun, or noun phrase. Some ideas:

Self-confidence
Prosperity
Peace of mind
Freedom (from _____)
Organization
Work independence
Optimism
Self-acceptance
Self-love
Delight
Strength (physical/mental/emotional)
Entertainment
A new marketable skill
Calm
Physical health
Mental health
A cherished possession
Sense of belonging
Resilience

STEP 3: Using 1 and 2 above, wrap your "why" around them
(10 minutes)

Now that you've heard your Listener's story and know both **a)** who they are and **b)** what they need most, let's talk about where their story might connect with yours.

To do that —and big thanks to Simon Sinek for teaching us all to think this way—we're going use this tailored adaptation of his simple "Why" formula:

> **I offer** (your product/service/offering)
> **SO THAT you can** (do/have/be this).

The "I" in the equation is you. The "you" in the equation is your Listener, the one you most want to have as a client, customer, reader, or supporter.

Why is this important? One issue with 90% of marketing is STILL that it ends the sentence after the first part: "I offer this." Sure, that tells me about your service or product, but it says nothing about how my life will be better for having worked with you. And that's critical.

By the way, for the purposes of this exercise, don't be tempted to change "you" to something else. This isn't an elevator speech. It's a story starter. You're talking to a human, not writing a generic flyer.

As an example, here's mine:

My Listener:
A purpose-driven entrepreneur who's passionate about his or her small business

My 'why' statement for them:
I offer guidance and hands-on services that help you promote your work with integrity, so that you can reach more of the right people and grow your business authentically.

Other examples:

Listener:
An individual living with a diagnosis of bipolar disorder

Why:
I offer resources, strategies, and coaching so that you can get your life and happiness back.
. . .

Listener:
An introverted leader in academia

Why:
I offer one-on-one mentoring so that you can communicate more naturally and effectively with the students who most need your help

Your turn:
Try a few of your own "why" statements until you find one that feels true and gives you a little inward smile.

STEP 4: Craft a bite-sized story to tell 30 minutes)

Choose from these easy-to-implement actions for your website, social media, or e-newsletter:

Reach out to at least one recent client by email.
Ask if they'd write a testimonial, review, or story about their positive experience. Consider making their task less daunting by asking them specific questions, such as:
What was an obstacle, concern, or worry that might have prevented you from initially contacting me? What did you find instead, as a result of getting to know my style and my work?
What specific part of working together did you like most? Would you recommend the particular service/product you chose to other people? If so, why?
Is there anything you'd like to say to someone who might be "on the fence"?

Share these on your website, social media, or as pull quotes in any marketing materials (after getting permission of course).

Search for an evocative picture that's "worth a thousand words."
Find an image that captures the mood & feeling your Listener may be carrying with them when they visit you online. Alternately, find an image of the feeling you

WANT them to carry after they've worked with you. I'm a fan of these sites for large-format images:

https://pixabay.com
https://pexels.com
https://unsplash.com

As an experiment, visit unsplash.com and type the word "relief" into the Search box at the top. You'll be able to parse through over 200 images. Each tells a visual story of relief, and in a way that's 100 times better than just typing "My clients feel relief after working with me" on a given page. Big bonus points if you can use a photo of an actual client for whom you've made an impact.

Share these images anywhere in the online spaces you frequent.

Write 100 meaningful words.
Make yourself human in the eyes of your clients, customers, and readers. Write 100 words about how you came to be doing the work you're doing. It can be a story about an obsession from your childhood, an incident in your circle of family and friends that moved you, a trauma that turned out to be a life-changer, or just how you feel when you do it.

Add it to your website's About or Home pages, or as a post to your Facebook business page if you have one, or as an article on your LinkedIn page, or anywhere else you have a presence online. Help us to know you.

We prefer to work with and buy from people who have a face and a story.

Here's a smattering of other kinds of bite-sized stories:

A Client Story:
All potential clients have a story they WANT to be moving into - one that's better than the one they're living today. Tell a story about how a specific client's life has been made better, healthier, more hopeful, or more beautiful. How has he worked to become a better version of himself? Use an alias if you need to, or get permission from a real client to tell their story.
Where to share it:
Website (home page, services/products/gallery page, about you page, sales page, blog)
Social media (Facebook business page with photo/video, Facebook groups, LinkedIn post, YouTube video, Instagram stories, Pixabay)
E-newsletter

A Thank You Story:
Say thank you to an employee, partner, client, supplier, even a competitor. Tell a short story about how they matter to you, why you're grateful, how being connected to them makes you feel. It's one thing to offer a good product or service; it's another to be the kind of person who says thanks for the good things in your life. People remember.
Where to share it:
Website (blog, an "our clients" page, about you page)

Social media (Facebook business page with photo, YouTube video, Instagram stories, Twitter, Pixabay) E-newsletter

A Hero Story:
Who is a hero in your work life? Who have you watched go from ordinary to extraordinary? Who has inspired you, and how? How can you help your client see herself as a hero in her own life – with the help of a wise mentor (you) offering liberating resources and knowledge?
Where to share it:
Website (blog, an "our clients" page, resources page)
Social media (Facebook business page with photo/video, link to a YouTube video, LinkedIn post) E-newsletter

A Goal Story:
What change are you hoping to make in the world, big or small, serious or funny? It could be something as simple as a beautiful set of photographs, or as serious as helping someone know himself better so his life is richer and fuller. Think about the challenges facing the people you most want to help. What are they? And how do you hope to use your work to banish them?
Where to share it:
Website (home page, blog, about you page)
Social media (Facebook business page, Facebook business page "about" description, Facebook groups, text on your Facebook cover banner, LinkedIn profile description, Twitter)
E-newsletter

A Story About What You Stand For

Is there a particular nonprofit or cause you support, perhaps one that ties in well with the work you do? Have you ever considered sharing this with your audience? If you donate a portion of your profits to this cause, for example, or if you volunteer, or sit on their board, it tells people what you stand for.

Where to share it:

Website (website footer on all pages, home page, blog, about you page)

Social media (Facebook business page AND personal profile with a link to the cause for visibility, LinkedIn profile description, Twitter, photos on Instagram, link to their YouTube explainer video)

E-newsletter

STEP 5: Get your stories posted and share them
(10 minutes)

If you have a Wordpress site, it's generally very easy and fast to add new text to a page wherever it's needed. Social media is even easier, if you already have the accounts set up.

If neither of these is true for you, you might want to use your Step 5 minutes to contact the person in your circle who makes that sort of thing happen for you. You can also contact me at https://websitesforgood.com for counsel or help, of course.

Once your story has been made public, be sure to let people know. If you have an email subscriber list, make it an excuse to contact subscribers and say hello. If you have a Facebook business page, consider an ad or boost to be sure it reaches the people you want to read it (ads can be VERY cheap and effective on Facebook).

I coach people through one-hour story jumpstart sessions, and also help them to set up outlets (sites, blogs, social media channels) on which to share them. Feel free to visit me at https://websitesforgood.com to learn more and say hello.

And above all:

Always, always, always keep looking out for opportunities to capture your own stories and share them.

14

WHAT'S *MY* STORY? ABOUT THE AUTHOR

To find something useful about myself to share with you, I was advised by a very smart person in my circles to go back and revisit the stories of my own life. With those in hand, she said, I'd be better able to write a sort of verbal video montage that would help you get to know me. To walk my talk, you know?

It's a risky approach in my case, as you'll see, but here goes:

Many of the frames you'd see from the young-girl part of that montage would be scary ones: Blurry dark-ocean images of fear, violence and grief. Then the imagery shifts, showing a young woman in a long sequence of escapes, strange journeys, far too much climbing and falling and bumps and bruises. The thing you'll notice most is the change in her over time. She smiles more each year. She's always studying some new topic rabidly, forever holding a textbook or on her way to a class, trusting that knowledge will be the sextant that will guide her to more sovereignty over her life.

Ta-daaah! Now you see Suit Girl, commuting every day to a cubicle, then an office, then a window office. She's escaped the dark oceans at last. Or has she?

Finally, you'll see the woman curled in the fetal position in the hallway of her suburban home, her blazer crumpled into a damp heap on the floor. Her fists clenched in pain. The kind doctor you see in blue scrubs in the next frame says pancreatitis. Suit Girl says, "Give me a pill so I can go back to work." The tired doctor shakes his head and says, "Change your life or the next time I see you, it'll be as a diabetic, or worse. You have a choice. Take it."

At that point, I'd shaken off my demons and survived to become a competent employee in mainstream business. Like so many, I'd worked for years for someone else's gain. I swapped 60+ hours of my life energy each week for an automatic deposit into my bank account. I dealt with stress, migraines, and chronic illness and I thought it was all just a part of normal life. That tired doctor was the turnaround point in my story, where I chose to leave that world, shut off autopilot, and start my own company, Websites for Good, so I could be part of something meaningful and lasting.

I still sometimes work long hours, but it rarely feels that way. In the two decades since then, I've talked with hundreds of people who carry different versions of the same story: They're stepping off the moving walkway of their lives to do work that gives them a stronger sense of purpose and connection, work that matters. I jump in with counsel to help them shape their business or practice, and help decipher online marketing tools to help them get the word out about what they offer the world.

Mostly though, I teach them how to stand out by sharing their own unique stories and learning the stories of the people they serve.

There's huge, wild energy in this, and I hope you're willing to give it a try, or if you're already there, to dive deeper.

So off you go. Some next steps:

So we're at the end of our time together. Here are some pint-sized actions you might consider doing next, just to keep in flow:

1. Start thinking about snippets of story that you think will help you be more real, more human, and more helpful to your clients. You can capture them in the **Storytelling for Small Business Workbook** at https://websitesforgood.com/workbook, or in a notebook that's just for that purpose

2. Go back to the **One-Hour Story Jumpstart** and choose one small step you can take this week.

3. Turn a couple of pages and dive into the Additional Resources to help build your own story toolkit. It's growing all the time.

4. Talk to me any time. Seriously, you can do that. I offer a free non-icky, no-sales-pitch conversation by phone, Skype, or Zoom so you can ask your burning questions. I'm not in the least bit stuffy or scary or salesy (but you knew that by now, right?) and I love helping people mine their gorgeous stories and build their businesses.

Whatever you choose to do, please drop me a note via any of the channels below, and let me know what you thought of the book, what you'd like to see more of/less of in the next edition, and how you're using it.

Because I'm looking forward to learning <u>your</u> story.

Margaret Rode
Small Business Coaching: https://margaretrode.com
Web Sherpa-ing: https://websitesforgood.com
Facebook: https://facebook.com/websitesforgood
Email: mrode@websitesforgood.com
Phone: 720.507.1893

15
STORYTELLING RESOURCES

Below you'll find a capture of the current resource list located on my website, which will undoubtedly change the minute I send this book off to the printer. But I wanted to provide some of my favorites here, and for an updated list, please go online to the Storytelling for Small Business Resource Bank here:

https://websitesforgood.com/storytelling-small-business-resources/

The Storytelling for Small Business Workbook

Do you have the Storytelling for Small Business Workbook yet? It's a great tool to start capturing and pondering your own stories, ideas, and observations. Download it here: https://websitesforgood.com/storytelling-for-small-business-workbook-2018/

My Articles and My Facebook Community

Because story endlessly fascinates me, I'm always talking about storytelling in some way. I invite you to read my blog posts about story and visit me on Facebook to join the conversation in either place. You can also contact me with any questions you may have, or topics you'd love to see covered.

Books

There are a lot of other books about business storytelling, but I shy away from many of them because of their manipulative nature. I'm interested in storytelling as a way to grow my business by creating solid, trusting relationships. So the ones that approach it purely from a place of coercion and sales (and you can generally tell those from their title/blurb) aren't as interesting to me.

My "keepers"
Here are some books about story that I've purchased, read, re-read, and recommend without reservation:

The Story Factor: Inspiration, Influence, and Persuasion Through the Art of Storytelling (2009 Edition)
Annette Simmons
Despite the use of "persuasion" in the title, this book is written from a place of genuine regard for relationships and connection. Full of stories and examples, and written in a very approachable and easy style, I find myself referring back to it often.

Long Story Short: The Only Storytelling Guide You'll Ever Need
Margot Leitman
A general storytelling guide from standup comedian, The Moth storytelling award winner, and business storytelling consultant, Margot Leitman. Although not technically a business book, the tools and how-to material in this very funny guide are valuable to all of us.

Business Storytelling for Dummies
Karen Dietz and Lori Silverman
This is a solid, easy-reading, comprehensive guidebook that helps with finding the stories of your business and figuring out where and when to tell them. A good reference guide for your bookshelf.

Others books you may enjoy
These are titles that have gems of wisdom in their own right, but check out the book description and reviews to be sure the subject matter and energy feels on-target for you:
Let the Story Do the Work by Esther Choy
The Storytelling Animal: How Stories Make Us Human by Jonathan Gottschall
Stories for Work: The Essential Guide to Business Storytelling by Gabrielle Dolan
Building a StoryBrand: Clarify Your Message So Customers Will Listen by Donald Miller
Tribes: We Need You to Lead Us by Seth Godin
Storytelling: The Indispensable Art of Entrepreneurism by Rudy Mazzocchi
Resonate: Present Visual Stories that Transform Audiences by Nancy Duarte
Wired for Story: The Writer's Guide to Using Brain Science to Hook Readers from the Very First Sentence: by Lisa Cron

Storytelling Podcasts

I often listen to podcasts while I'm working, while exercising, while walking the dog...I find them a great way to get in some extra learning time and also a way to help with the isolation that solo entrepreneurs can sometimes feel. Here are some of my favorites:

Podcasts about business storytelling in specific:

The Business of Story Podcast with Park Howell
https://businessofstory.com/storytelling-podcast/
Long-running podcast with something for every businessperson. Named to the top 40 Small Business Podcasts in 2017, this business storytelling podcast draws from a diverse collection of guest wisdom to curate tips, tools, and strategies to help your marketing stand out.

STORY from StoryGatherings.com
https://storygatherings.com/podcast
Weekly inspiration and creative tips for makers, small businesspeople, artists, and storytellers, with the goal of inspiring us all to "do our best, most meaningful work."

Be The Drop – Investigating Brand Storytelling with Amelia Veale
http://narrativemarketing.com.au/categories/be-the-drop/
This podcast focuses on "communication that connects, unites and generates engagement." Guests include CEOs, Olympians, not-for-profit directors, social media gurus, and more, to discover how they use story to connect with their community.

Build a StoryBrand Podcast with Donald Miller
https://buildingastorybrand.com/blog/
Super-interesting guests like Dan Pink, Dan Heath, Seth Godin, Amy Porterfield, Michael Hyatt, and dozens more

make this podcast a valuable companion to my daily workout (I've learned to keep a pen and paper handy...) Inspiring and practical advice on clarifying your message and growing your business using the power of story.

[Anecdotally Speaking Podcast](#) with Anecdote.com
https://www.anecdote.com/podcasts/
A new podcast in 2018, Anecdote aims to help us all become a great business storyteller and build a repertoire of stories we can tell to engage, influence and inspire. Join Shawn Callahan and Mark Schenk from Anecdote as they share great stories to tell, why they work and when to tell them.

Podcasts about storytelling in general:

[This American Life](#) with Ira Glass
https://www.thisamericanlife.org/
A weekly public radio show, heard by 2.2 million people on more than 500 stations. Another 2.5 million people download the weekly podcast. It is hosted by Ira Glass, produced in collaboration with Chicago Public Media, delivered to stations by PRX The Public Radio Exchange, and has won all of the major broadcasting awards. I rarely miss it.

[Revisionist History](#) with Malcolm Gladwell
http://revisionisthistory.com/
Revisionist History is bestselling author Malcolm Gladwell's journey through the overlooked and the misunderstood. Every episode re-examines something from the past—an event, a person, an idea, even a song—and asks whether we got it right the first time. A fascinating trip with a master storyteller.

The Moth Radio Hour and Podcast

https://www.themoth.org/

Since its launch in 1997, The Moth has presented thousands of true stories to standing-room-only crowds worldwide. Moth storytellers stand alone, under a spotlight, with only a microphone and a roomful of strangers. Looking for something to plug into your ears while walking or exercising? The varied length and themes of The Moth shows make it a perfect companion.

StoryCorps

https://storycorps.org/podcast/

StoryCorps started in 2003 with the opening of a story booth in New York's Grand Central Terminal. Since then, it has collected and archived nearly 75,000 facilitated interviews from more than 150,000 participants from across the country who visit one of its recording sites. It is one of the largest oral history projects of its kind. It has grown into an enduring national institution that—I hope—fosters a culture of listening in the United States. The podcast is an utter delight.

Thought-Provoking Articles

This list is growing constantly...I have a backlog of hundreds that I'm endeavoring to share here. I'll put the most recent ones at the top, and as the list grows I'll break it out into categories. (having a surplus of stimulating reading material is a good problem to have, isn't it?)

More Stories Means More Readers (Plus, 15 Stories You Should Be Telling)

http://storybistro.com/more-stories-more-readers/
StoryBistro.com, 11 January 2018

The 5 Elements of Storytelling Every Entrepreneur Needs to Know
https://www.entrepreneur.com/article/270049
by Matthew Toren, *Entrepreneur.com*, 28 January 2016

The Power of Storytelling: How We Got 300% More People To Read Our Content
https://blog.bufferapp.com/power-of-story
by Alex Turnbull on *BufferApp.com*, 22 April 2014

Why Our Brains Crave Storytelling In Marketing
https://www.fastcompany.com/3031419/why-our-brains-crave-storytelling-in-marketing
by Rachel Gillett, *FastCompany.com*, 4 June 2014

16
BIG THANKS

Somehow, even though I'm introverted, nerdy, and ever-so-slightly socially awkward, I've found myself part of a community full of smart, funny, and big-hearted people trying to make some sort of difference in the world with the time they're given. How did I get so lucky?

To all of my clients, friends, and family members who put up with my long disappearances and radio silence while I worked on my first book, I send along my gratitude and the promise of coffee together as soon as I'm done.

To my incredibly tolerant husband, thank you for all your love and support, and for those beers that magically appeared at my elbow during late night writing sessions. Oh, and also for taking the dog out when I was lost in edits. And to Gordon the Dog, how are you even reading this without opposable thumbs? Don't tell me you learned to swipe?

To all the brilliant and busy humans who took time away from their OWN work to listen to me babble about storytelling, or to read the book, or to critique book titles and covers and endless tables of contents, or to just say "keep going," I am deeply in your debt. Thanks again to:

Kathleen Adams, Center for Journal Therapy, and the Journalverse

http://journaltherapy.com, http://twinstitute.net and
http://journalverse.com
Christina Baldwin, Peerspirit Inc.
http://peerspirit.com

Judith Morgan and the Small Business Big Magic gang
http://judithmorgan.com

George Kao and his 2017 and 2018 Masterheart Groups
http://georgekao.com

Noelle Sterne Ph.D
http://trustyourlifenow.com

Barbara Stahura
http://barbarastahura.com

Leia Francisco
http://leiafrancisco.com

Katy Moses Huggins
http://katymoses.com

Elaine Brooks
http://mypathtochange.com

Simon Berkowitz
http://samaii.com

Rochelle Melander
http://writenowcoach.com

Rose Diamond
http://tribeintransition.net

You're the best and I love you all.